GIGANOTOSAURUS

BY REBECCA SABELKO

EPIC

BELLWETHER MEDIA • MINNEAPOLIS, MN

EPIC BOOKS are no ordinary books. They burst with intense action, high-speed heroics, and shadows of the unknown. Are you ready for an Epic adventure?

This edition first published in 2022 by Bellwether Media, Inc.

No part of this publication may be reproduced in whole or in part without written permission of the publisher. For information regarding permission, write to Bellwether Media, Inc., Attention: Permissions Department, 6012 Blue Circle Drive, Minnetonka, MN 55343.

Library of Congress Cataloging-in-Publication Data

Names: Sabelko, Rebecca, author.
Title: Giganotosaurus / by Rebecca Sabelko.
Description: Minneapolis, MN : Bellwether Media, 2022. | Series: The world of dinosaurs |
Includes bibliographical references and index. | Audience: Ages 7-12 | Audience: Grades 2-3 |
Summary: "Engaging images accompany information about giganotosaurus. The combination of
 high-interest subject matter and light text is intended for students in grades 2 through 7"-- Provided by publisher.
Identifiers: LCCN 2021022419 (print) | LCCN 2021022420 (ebook) | ISBN 9781644875445 (library binding) |
 ISBN 9781648345005 (paperback) | ISBN 9781648344527 (ebook)
Subjects: LCSH: Giganotosaurus--Juvenile literature.
Classification: LCC QE862.S3 S23243 2022 (print) | LCC QE862.S3 (ebook) | DDC 567.912--dc23
LC record available at https://lccn.loc.gov/2021022419
LC ebook record available at https://lccn.loc.gov/2021022420

Editor: Betsy Rathburn   Designer: Jeffrey Kollock

Printed in the United States of America, North Mankato, MN

TABLE OF CONTENTS

THE WORLD OF THE GIGANOTOSAURUS

JEE-guh-NOH-toh-SAWR-us

The giganotosaurus was huge!
It was one of the biggest meat-eating
dinosaurs to ever live.

MAP OF THE WORLD

Late Cretaceous period

It lived around 100 million years ago during the **Cretaceous period**. This was during the **Mesozoic era**.

WHAT WAS THE GIGANOTOSAURUS?

The giganotosaurus stretched over 45 feet (13.7 meters) long.

It weighed over 17,000 pounds (7,711 kilograms). That is about as much as four large hippos!

NAME GAME

The word *giganotosaurus* means "giant southern lizard."

SIZE CHART

25 feet (7.6 meters)	
15 feet (4.6 meters)	
5 feet (1.5 meters)	

This **theropod** moved on two legs. Its long tail helped it balance. It ran at speeds around 30 miles (48 kilometers) per hour!

clawed
fingers

The dinosaur had two short arms.
Each hand had three clawed fingers.

BANANA BRAIN

The giganotosaurus's head grew up to 6 feet (1.8 meters) long. But its brain was tiny. It was about the same size and shape as a banana!

The giganotosaurus was a "shark-toothed" dinosaur. It had serrated teeth like many sharks.

The dinosaur's teeth grew up to
8 inches (20 centimeters) long!
They easily sliced through prey.

DIET AND DEFENSES

The giganotosaurus was a mighty **predator**. Scientists believe it hunted long-necked dinosaurs. It was one of the few dinosaurs that did.

It may have hunted in **packs**. The dinosaurs surrounded their prey so it could not escape.

GIGANOTOSAURUS DIET

rotting meat

Argentinosaurus

The dinosaurs attacked one by one.
They bit into their prey's flesh.
They slashed with their sharp claws.

⚠ BIG DINO, BIG PREY

Scientists believe the giganotosaurus
hunted the Argentinosaurus.
This dinosaur grew up to 10 times
larger than the giganotosaurus!

Even the biggest prey was no match for a giganotosaurus pack!

FOSSILS AND EXTINCTION

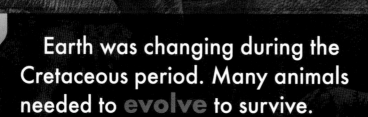

Earth was changing during the Cretaceous period. Many animals needed to **evolve** to survive.

The giganotosaurus could
not adapt. It went extinct.

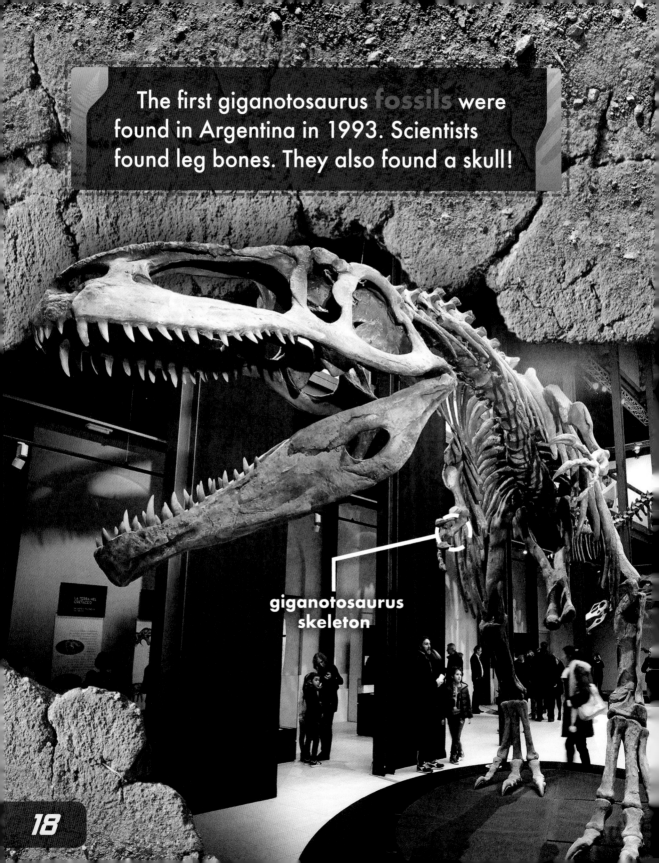

The first giganotosaurus fossils were found in Argentina in 1993. Scientists found leg bones. They also found a skull!

giganotosaurus
skeleton

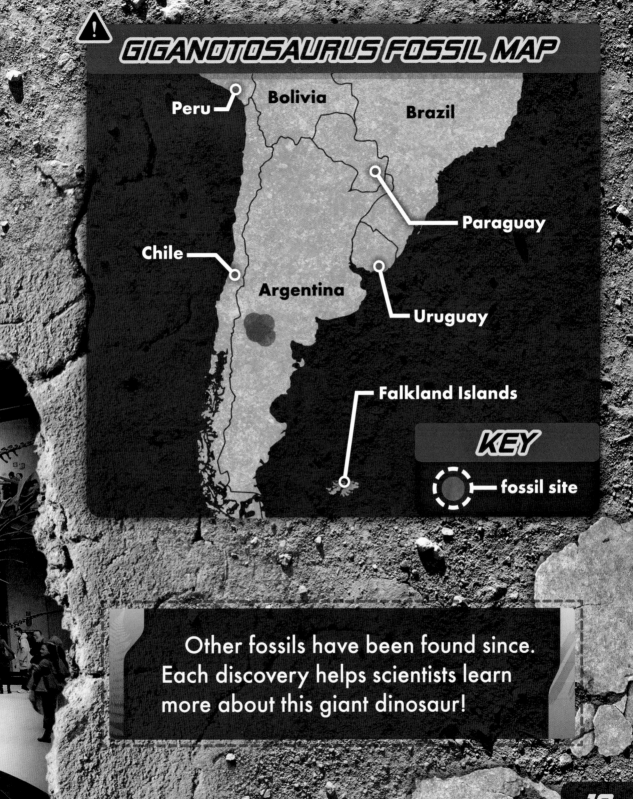

GIGANOTOSAURUS FOSSIL MAP

Peru

Bolivia

Brazil

Paraguay

Chile

Argentina

Uruguay

Falkland Islands

KEY

fossil site

Other fossils have been found since. Each discovery helps scientists learn more about this giant dinosaur!

GET TO KNOW THE GIGANOTOSAURUS

serrated teeth

HEIGHT around 15 feet (4.6 meters) tall at the hip

⚠️ **LOCATION**

South America

3 claws on each hand

LENGTH up to 45 feet (13.7 meters) long

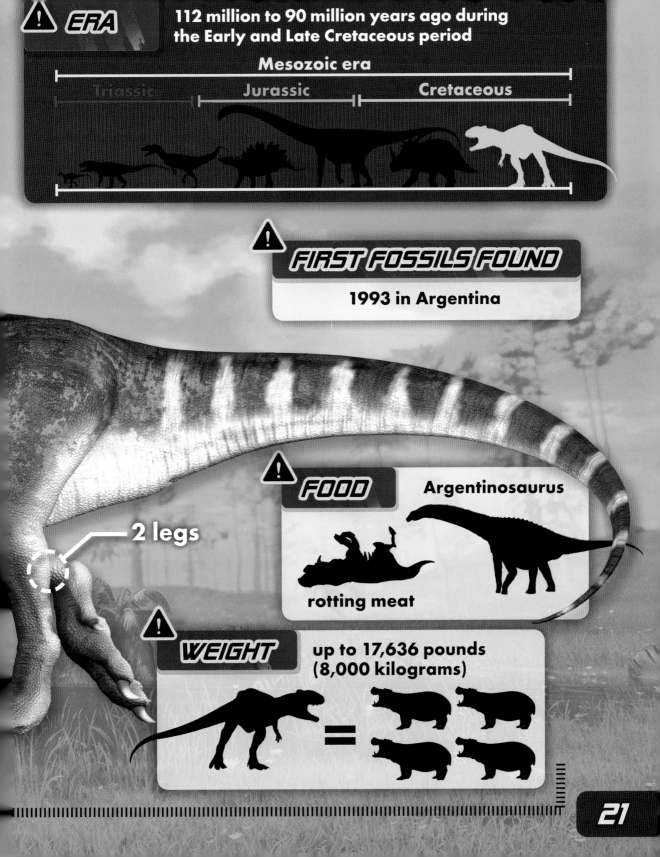

⚠ FIRST FOSSILS FOUND

1993 in Argentina

2 legs

⚠ FOOD

rotting meat

Argentinosaurus

⚠ WEIGHT

up to 17,636 pounds (8,000 kilograms)

=

GLOSSARY

adapt—to change to fit different conditions

Cretaceous period—the last period of the Mesozoic era that occurred between 145 million and 66 million years ago

evolve—to change slowly, often into a better, more complex state

extinct—no longer living

fossils—the remains of living things that lived long ago

Mesozoic era—a time in history in which dinosaurs lived on Earth; the first birds, mammals, and flowering plants appeared on Earth during the Mesozoic era.

packs—groups of the same animals; giganotosaurus may have hunted in packs.

predator—an animal that hunts other animals for food

prey—animals hunted by other animals for food

serrated—having a sawlike edge

theropod—a meat-eating dinosaur that had two small arms and moved on two legs

TO LEARN MORE

AT THE LIBRARY

Howell, Izzi. *Dino-sorted!: Killer (Theropod) Dinosaurs.*
London, England: Hachette Children's Group, 2021.

Sabelko, Rebecca. *Argentinosaurus.* Minneapolis, Minn.:
Bellwether Media, 2021.

Sabelko, Rebecca. *Tyrannosaurus Rex.* Minneapolis, Minn.:
Bellwether Media, 2020.

ON THE WEB

FACTSURFER

Factsurfer.com gives you
a safe, fun way to find
more information.

1. Go to www.factsurfer.com.

2. Enter "giganotosaurus" into the search box
   and click 🔍.

3. Select your book cover to see a list
   of related content.

INDEX